Adam Aitken | Eighth Habitation

New Poems

GIRAMONDO POETS

Adam Aitken | Eighth Habitation

First published 2009
for the Writing & Society Research Group
at the University of Western Sydney
by the Giramondo Publishing Company
PO Box 752 Artarmon NSW 1570 Australia
www.giramondopublishing.com

Designed by Harry Williamson
Typeset by Andrew Davies
in 10/16.75 pt Baskerville

Printed and bound by Ligare Book Printers
Distributed in Australia by Tower Books

National Library of Australia
Cataloguing-in-Publication data:

Aitken, Adam 1960 –
Eighth Habitation / Adam Aitken

ISBN 978-1-920882-46-4

1. Title

A821.3

For Neela Griffiths

Previous Collections

Letter To Marco Polo
In One House
Crossing Lake Toba (chapbook)
Romeo and Juliet in Subtitles
Impermanence.com (chapbook)

This project has been assisted by the Commonwealth Government through the Australia Council, its arts funding and advisory body.

Acknowledgements

I would like to thank the editors of: *The Age*, *Asia Literary Review* (Hong Kong), *Australian Literary Review*, *Best Australian Poetry 2004*, *Best Australian Poems 2005*, *Chautauqua Literary Journal* (USA), *Cordite*, *Dotlit*, *Drunken Boat* (USA), *Famous Reporter*, *Gangway*, *Griffith Review*, *Heat*, *Jacket*, *Mascara*, *Overland*, *Perfume River* (Vietnam), *Peril*, *Poetry Espresso*, *Poetry International.org*, *Poetry Without Borders*, *Poets Against War: Poets Union Anthology*, *Qarrtsiluni*, *Quarterly Literary Review Singapore*, *Said the Rat!*, *Salt-lick Quarterly*, *Tinfish* (USA), *Trout*, *Writing Macao*, and *Impermanence.com* (Vagabond).

This book would not have been possible without the advice and encouragement of Fiona Wright, Greg McLaren, Niobe Syme, Adrian Wiggins, Jane Gibian, Liz Allen, Michael Brennan, Michelle Cahill, and Pam Brown. I am especially grateful to Viki Holmes, for her close editing.

The sequence 'Cambodian poems' could not have been written without the Literature Board of the Australia Council, whose support enabled me to live in Cambodia in 2008.

Also, thanks to Ivor Indyk and Evelyn Juers for their unstinting support over the years.

Contents

Broken / Unbroken

Fin de Siècle

Between two climates she'd be waiting, the slender
young emigré
so dark and delicate the wind passed right through her,
always there before you, the bright architect of love
who knew her way around the café chairs, the Latin lovers.
How she'd inspired that horizon, the penthouse, the tower.
Greek, French, Ukrainian, all of the above? No-one knew
for sure
what drove her south one winter, a whim or a storm.
Her age or why she had promised to see you again,
or why she always promised, sighing, mood-wracked,
hat wide-brimmed with daisies and gliding towards you
through the fun palace colonnades before sunset –
no-one knew
why she always promised to be there
under the whitewash crumbling, that left its stain
on your waiter's apron and in your hair, as if you
had emerged
unscathed from its collapse, the blast driving you back,
grasping your last tip. Broken and unbroken
she would arrive after work (though no-one knew
what she did),
complement your menu, then a final swim
before the chill shadows enclosed the beach.
Statues murmured in the dusk,
and in the bracelet of a rockpool children sparkled

among their castles, before they flooded at high tide.
Were they her children? If so they could never be
    too careful
building their moats, before she moved to a bench
    in the sun.
The Latin lovers waved and she didn't wave back.
She was the pleasure of the world passing, about to shake
her wings free of the disaster, and take off, and leave you
once again thinking this had been the best century ever
and you were haunted by what she could not forget,
already beyond your knowing, what she is and was.

Fable

That year they rode low in the water
on a ballast of oaths and convicted emotions

moved on to springtime ports
past the Pig and Sows reef
and the ridiculously expensive prison
lost steerage in a lull of unconcern
and absent-minded fishing.

In those days an invasion
was a kind of plague jellyfish
or cold front
that blew in early, unseasonal.
    Everyone was hitching rides.
When someone entered
new seasons of exchange – fluids, fire,
language and metal –
someone else exited.
They were what they made, and what they
couldn't
someone else did.
Another's lack seemed
no more than their own.
All land codified

as the visible,
scoured and clearfelled,
great land
of the forever language.

At Rozelle Asylum

At Rozelle Asylum, his final destination.
The quartermaster who'd cracked
          drew
on a sandstone pier
a worldly fish, a navy frigate in its port,

a tropic bird of seed.
Full sails, great promise,
a kind of escape
from a madder Captain.

The botanist inside
who made the book for all,
engraved, exotic
with his names – each new flower and tree

and new stiff Latin, the whole evolutionary kit,
the iron bars of genealogy.

Doctor, I ask you: what inky blot liberates
or draws us together
between the covers of hand-bound books
when we want a name and legacy
to crown the sky?

Fig trees, for instance, just
appear between the stones, green
as immigrants or refugees
hidden in the shade.

Are they natives now by instant decree?
You wear their leafy heads, and see
yourself once again,
historical footnote, crazed misfit

scattered, afraid, frozen
in unseasonal rain,
wasted now, due to
lack of name or use: seedy fruit
scattered in the grass,

import that multiplied.
What of the bigger machines, like
destiny, meaning, sanity?
The fork and divergences
of who we want to be?
The rigging
on your ship
will catch the breeze, then turn
and catch it once again.

A Biography of 13

with a line by Wisława Szymborska

And so the tour begins and ends:
'The North Sea wind blew across the Belgian mud
the flames rose in the German east.'
Huddled in memory's dispatch box
Major Aitken buttoned up
his 13th Light Horse tunic.
No disgrace, he'd made it back,
from sniping Johnny Turk
to traffic duty at the Somme
to desk jockey on the Salisbury Plain,
signing off on casualties,
supervising bayonet drills.
At ANZAC shrines in Melbourne
he'd pray with Presbyterian attention
and drink like the rest,
his medals catching the sun.

I swig a VB, the brand his father founded,
millionaire brewer
who left behind 13 children
and a will as long as this book.
I think of those to whom
the medals filter down.

13 years after V Day my father went to Singapore
and bargained with a waif at Changi
for 13 postcards, 'so cheap'
he just *had* to buy them.
His talents were letters, logistics,
advertising copy, wearing suits.
At the Office Party in Bangkok
he danced, quite pissed, in women's lace
then swapped the Major's 'lucky' digger hat
for a set of Dutch clogs.

When I was 13 my father left home.
Now I dream of a salt ghost
and recall the correct timing
for bells to ring, the melody for reveille
and other regimental habits
like whistles, or the cordite reek
of explosions, or what could make
the trench diorama more interactive
'when all the cameras
have gone to other wars'.
I think of how to honour a tattooed grazier
who became an auditor of destruction;
how he went to hell and back again
like a number 13 horse (better than 8)
running on the luck they say it never brings.

Ionian

are war and peace
playing their little game over your dead body?
Jorie Graham

Eastern Asian time, he arrived
at the cove.
Small figures camped in ruined hills,
waiting to advance.
He had his horse, high rank
and a point of view,
timetables and maps: each hill,
on the coordinates to fame,
the minefield, the track
to that strategic
hilltop village, a tour guide,
and parking for officers.

Ninety years on, sons of snipers
fish on the quiet beach, sipping
hot mint tea.
The winning cavalry
rents out donkeys,
for a few lira
escorts you through the ruins.

Tides regroup
and the opalescent waters

whet a TV crew's Byronic taste
for filigreed pistols and broken columns.

Filling the boat with trench-booty;
a gorgeous sunset, or the exact
scent of victory
too subtle for my words.

Discoveries Made Collecting Botanic Samples

My mind aslant with your haunting
they said that you'd been thrown
off the edge,
whom I imagined I once knew.
My run to the usual lookout
marked now by your shadow.
My emptying began:
      recycled, tidal, grief but not quite grief at all
to half-forget, to pause
at the wild nasturtiums, and forage
for the rare harlequin octopus
hiding in rocks, turning itself purple, green
or a more lethal blue.

Out there, or within your mind,
camouflaged or not, cruising your memory
I remember you, not as fish, but
the imprint of a fish
long gone from its fishbowl.
How I swam toward it,
      the groper of Clovelly
before it drifted off, legend of the bay.

Your absence, like Sydney humidity, still curls
this postcard I wanted to send;
no-one knows your address.

Cormorants preening for parasites.
My thoughts a row of flats
    blocking everyone's view.
How then to claim the glittering window
or afford the membership fee?
Seabirds aim for a pilchard shoal.
The killers have multiple heads of ambition.
Aztecs stole your peasant heart,
you served the demon's purpose,
the octopus found your shoes.

You'd gone off duty, to cruise, to sail
relieved of dishes and endless orders for Thai fishcake
and more sauce. By morning they'd found you,
a stain on the cliff face
that faded in a brief shower.
The city so rare and speechless
where you lie
unnamed, between the inexorable layers.

To My Double

Even my beautiful other half
reminds me of you

We are growing old
at a simultaneous pace

We both take
the exact half of the first

bottle of wine
After that the wisdom-ratio

is pure astronomy

We watch the same programs
and laugh together

You used to pick the murderer
first

now I do

We cry together too
when once it was only

one half that cried
the other stony faced

Now our teeth
engage perfectly

We kiss much more
and for longer

On retirement
we know exactly

what we want to see
Love is a kind of

intense plot awareness
I look at myself

I see you

The Anti-travel Travel Poem

The anti-travel travel poem suggests the road
romance & regrets
the endless paperwork we left behind
I dreamed of walking boots that wouldn't lace
anti-travellers can never get lost
in a swamp of Choice we must take
the American grid pattern endless
military runways, the borders
of Empire, take-off zone & rabbit fence
keeping peace at the ruined city gate
where crows consider life in a decommissioned bomber
the line I have lain too long on the beach
staring at the awesome winter surf
is prelude to destruction & creation
the anti-travel travel poem does not
ask for directions on a road no-one's taken
it is arrested time at a six-ways crossroad
where cremation crews shoulder the Prince's corpse
malicious hangers-on decide it's time to quit
and humans go on burning quietly
find shelf space in a Singapore of metaphysics
food halls where no-one's lost
no-one's found, no-one needs directions
each well meant instruction (go straight
through the cemetery, turn left – or was it right?)

leads to the wilderness of whole new forests
wholly dedicated to paper (show us your ID, Dr Death!)
Sure not everyone's perfectly matched
even the President preferred golf,
the curve & arrow of ball and club, the flagged
plantation we thought would abolish
inter-island piracy forever, & snakes
that hide in elephant grass all know
how dangerous the sedentary life
being cute & poisonous at the same time
exiles mistaken for natives
non-travellers who decide to stay
feral & primitive, go loose, develop the local accent
camp on the edge of what they know best:
abandoned village with Pepsi sign
a dog dozing in a broken down truck
in the mountain's two thousand metre air
the sign on a frog statue
SORRY, NO ROOM SERVICE
hasn't changed since Eisenhower's visit
a red stop sign marks disused
industrial estate no-one but a film crew stops at
checkpoints for the apprentice guide
and even the ICBM stalls
on a one-way track to Krakatoa
with human maps it cannot read

rivers stop, flow back, released
from the burden of their own
meanderings, the drunk boatmen, Ophelias
overgrown bloated with silt, good for growing moss
from that moment a bird dropped seed
of grass & trees on no-where-in-particular's
shady undergrowth & the poem's farms & gardens
revert to shaggy Edens where no-one is a stranger
in a Kingdom of minute-by-minute ritual
where we know belonging, we know how.

To a Cyborg

Lie and tell me you are human.
Grace me perfectly.
Offspring of Nietzsche's tears
what sport fast enough
suits your pulse? Doubtless
you are mean & beatific, machine of paradox.
You look homely as a tank,
oiled god in intricate shoes
guzzling a viscous tonic.
I buy the magazine, and you are there –
burnished titanium, whippy carbon-fibre,
geared evolution of futile improvements.
Deep breather, with your rat-heart pump
your circuitry, your speeches,
isometric kestrel gliding for mice.
Let me grow you like a business,
heat-moulded from ancestral scrap
shaped on the wind's lathe, oh legislate
and open sesame you are there.
My laser blunts on you
body jigsawed from a slab.
The rest shall wait, and I fear
your needle, that swoon I thought
immortal.

If I have peaked too early,
sweat and say my lines, will you
lie with me fake tiger?
Are you mine?

First Contact

in memoriam A. C.

There are only so many ways to describe it:
chance meeting outside subway entrance in Paris,
coin I borrowed for a phone call,
the street kid who lit your cigarette.
Friend of friend at cocktail party!
Yes, the gorgeous friend with the plain chaperone.
Take your pick they are all fictions
some more beautiful than others.
You were just a 'shire girl',
straight out of movies.
Someone Irish who came ashore, armed and dangerous
after six months out at sea.
Yes, I liked that too, what a
coincidence I didn't think
anyone was interested.
Or was it mostly
your curly / my dark hair
your / my Irish temperament?
Where did we file your prize-poem?
Under 'Greece'? Under 'cafés'.
Your husband's favourite.
How unpromising that first house,
the musty carpet
and the cheap cask wine
I emptied that night.

Your housemate the opera soprano
scoffed chocolates and guffawed.
My stripped-down racing bike
never did fit that hallway.
We could hardly move, we moved.
You wanted forests. I didn't.
Your life so crowded I had to leave.

Force Zero

for Alan Jefferies

I

the waves flatten out to ripples on our breath
suntan lotion pearls the water

both surface and suntan
inflect prisms in the morning light

we blink as it stares us in the face

the heart beats out the days
blended through these fountain-pen desires
made foundation for our skins

so troublesome, this skin
so many bodies

the message of the surface
is joy squared, exponential!

all around there are the beautiful,
naked, tattooed, proud

do my looking for me
you say,

and I look for you
swimming into the West, celebrating

this remission from care
in our 'days of azure'

2

on this blemished horizon
shambolic real estate no-one owns
I think of cells gone wild
sucking up resources

I think of your
coded poems, your demi-monde

I think of you
mutating in the sun

I think of becoming
a small minor god

a miniature god of mutation
or a god of small things

as Arundati Roy puts it
in her mini-epic of small Indian things

the almost-whisper of a zero wind
promises good things

the way Christmas morning was
silence worth unwrapping

like Polynesians we sink down
into our earth our oceans

unlike Polynesians
we make metaphors of Polynesians

because the word is beautiful
and Polynesians are beautiful

a pearl diver's heart skips a beat
the ghost in the machine

a film of bubbles
rises up from the hidden reef

God? the pearl diver asked
but I never found Him
what pearl does not wrap itself in a shell?

there is nothing deeper

I thought of Lorca and
your duende
and the duende of Dulwich Hill
and knew it suited you

like a battered sports coat
that reeks of ganja
in that brasserie in Barcelona

– how Paradise threw out the poets
as dusk shut down like a shop

I remembered Machado's last stand
in a forties film noir

and we were purified
in Tzara's
'bath of circular landscapes'

Yes, it was so
but the doubt remains:

if you were dead
would I know you

would I know you perfectly?
In a mood

of revolutionary happiness
despite everything, the virus

wave never breaks
and the body wavering

is alive and remains just so

that zero
wind in my heart.

The Fire Watchers: A Memoir (in the Sydney Style)

Too blind to be a fireman, too flat footed
you sought out fires, big ones, coming home
late from school – and became
a heavy smoker of select Virginia.
But me who biked the Harbour Bridge
saw that playground burn,
Luna Park, its fretwork temple, the ghost train
razed, parents and children, fairy floss and chewing gum
gone to ash and blackout.
Mum who always turned away
had hoped I hadn't looked...

In the city he would always love
my father would slow to procession pace,
passing accident scenes.
I asked a lot of questions then, a kid stuck on 'Why?'
Obsessive, thirteen, and forensic I could memorise
the number injured, type of vehicle, angles of incidence.
Years before crumple zones,
crash dummies or digital instruments.
Brother, you were pool shark and surfing shaman,
who'd mimic sirens and I noted with skilled
Conservatorium training
how they differed – in pitch and rhythm –
from foreign ones on TV.

Like Dad you'd calm your nerves
with a lighter and a smoke, and watch the way he steered
knees on the wheel as he lit up,
the life we learned from America.

Reaching forty now I ask: why my mother
would never sew the hems of my jeans, even if Death
    on the TV
reminded her of us.
Who bought the photo albums, the biscuit tins
stacked and smiling? Now I've had them catalogued
the narratives refine themselves
with every passing year.

What exactly did we save?
On the day she burned his books I thought
how modern she'd become,
hard as a fallen city's final hour.
The pyramid glowed orange
then the pages curled – biographies, murder mysteries –
winged histories made permanent in print:
'50s crime classics, adulterous romance
well-plotted paperbacks he would have hoarded
if only to browse, somewhere between accounts,
reading his life away
in a balmy Sydney autumn.

Diary, March 18, 1956

Pethebridge drinks like a fish, and Hong Kong food's nothing like the chow food you get in Melbourne, and if you don't use chopsticks you don't eat. Pethebridge and I take a taxi to a Cabaret club in Kowloon. Danced with my first Asian: Carly, 19, a taxi dancer who goes to school where she learns English and other European subjects. Like all the other dancers, she wants me to teach her English. She has a slim figure and is quite beautiful. Hong Kong: a place full of lousy colonial Brits.

———

2 pr trousers – v. good (light colours) 1 Dacron about $20 (A 35/–)
4 shirts – 2 about $12 (each) v. good (A 9/6)
– 2 about $18 each, 1 Dacron & Cotton; 1 Silk (pure) (A 32/– ea)

———

Eleanor Kwong, commercial artist at Cathay Ltd. Talented artist, but temperamental! Works too hard. Great to go shopping with for clothes.

Bangkok, 5/04/57. A night with the girls at the Taxi Dance Club. One hour for 250 ticals.

Maude Couire, daughter of the French consul in Bangkok. A terrific girl of 19. Fabulous figure, great fun. Completely unsophisticated and very natural. Have become good friends and went to the pictures several times, but nothing more.

Noël Bulke, one of the nicest girls I've ever met. Daughter of Pakistani Ambassador. Noël is Anglo-Indian and she and Maude are very good friends – almost inseparable. A beautiful girl who has been all over the world. Completely unspoiled and natural. The way I like my women. Terrific fun but has more poise and personality than most girls 10 years her senior. Will make somebody a good wife.

October 7th, Bangkok. Edith Atkinson: daughter of a Thai-Malaysian and Dutch mother. The father is a wealthy accountant who has Anglicised his name. Edith intends to study Home Economics at a Melbourne college. Solid, lovely girl but not exciting. Very Europeanised, which is a good thing. Insisted I take her to watch taxi dancers. Probably has a dark side I have yet to experience.

———

'York Pub', Singapore, Christmas 1957

Xmas Menu:

1. Grapefruit Cocktail

2. Mushroom Soup

3. Fried Fillet of Sole

4. Roast Turkey, Ham, Forcemeat, Bread Sauce, Baked and Boiled Spuds, Green Peas

5. Christmas Pudding

6. Biscuits and Cheese

7. Fruit

8. Coffee

We also had Red or/and White Wine, Beer, and Gold Tipped Cigarettes.

And the meal was really fabulous.

———

Boxing Day; a day of recovery.
Next day: Tony and his Malay girlfriend Maria take me to the Tiger Balm Gardens.
Then to the 'Seventh Story' nightclub, where I teach Maria to dance,
as Tony has not had much success.
To Arthur's place, where we resumed the grog.
'Cockpit', a rather expensive and exclusive nightclub.

We had just started dinner when 1958 arrived.

———

Diary

New Years Day: rather quiet.

Went to see 'Teahouse of the August Moon' with S.

(I think I am in love with an Oriental!)

02/01/58: Slept in.

U.S. Coffee	4 oz	Tics (ticals) 16.00
U.S. Tomato Sauce	14 oz	Tics 12.00
U.S. Jam	12 oz	Tics 10.00
Marmite	4 oz	Tics 10.00
Local Eggs	1 doz	Tics 10.00 (4/2 doz)
Sugar (local)	1 lb	Tics 8.00
	I think (that's cube sugar)	
Australian butter	1 lb.	Tics 22.00!!

Aust. Bacon (enough for four days) Tics 10.00

~~American~~ Aust. Sausages (8) Tics 10.00

(very small and taste lousy)

New Straits Times, February 2nd, 1958

New Muslim Weds English Girl in Double Ceremony at Ipoh

Inche Johari marries Margaret Elaine ('Noraini') Cockshaw, aged 20 years. Che Noraini who now wears a sarong and kebaya is busy learning to speak Malay, getting used to the climate and learning to prepare curries.

Page 9: *The colonial secretary tells us what makes an ideal secretary.*

Page 10: *Rice and Spice: new ways of cooking rice.*

———

That night went out to the Dollar-a-Dance night club and met Singapore models – with roses in their hair – at the Chinese swimming club.

New Straits Times, February 16th:
Thailand's leader, Marshal Sarit, flies to Washington for an operation on his spleen.

Drop us a Line page:
Dear Sir,
Don't you think it is a shame that such a talented artiste as Elvis Presley
should have to do national service?
Signed 'Rock 'N' Roll, Singapore.

Dear Rock 'N' Roll
We reckon it will be the making of him if he stays

on in the army
for another 20 or 30 years.
We reckon that would be a wonderful thing too!

Dear Sir,
I am writing an essay on the Royal Navy during the war.
Could you please tell me what its losses were?
Ronny.

Dear Ronny,
51 thousand dead, 14,678 wounded
and 730 ships sunk.

'Happiest Story of the Week':
Malayan Couple Find Love in a World of Silence
Two deaf mute rubber tappers married today.
They were Cheng Siong Lim, 28, and Chan Lay Hua, 22, of Ayer Tawar.

———

Diary
If time I just HAVE to read the new novel
by Ramsay Ullmann, *Windon's Way*,
about a Malay Eurasian nurse
who marries an English doctor.

Read, or go to Airways House for cocktail party?'

(Two hours later)
Decide to go to the Chalerm Review Theatre,
where 'girls freeze men with hot strip-dances,
and Rose Chann (sic) performs her Hawaii Review,
and wrestles with 150 pound pythons.'

(Six hours later)
'Tired after another night out.
In bed approx. 2:30 AM.'

———

London, 1960
KODAK PLUS X B & N WFS 64 – 28.8.60

1. Adam	*3' 6'*	*F 5.6*	*100*	*underex.*
2. "	*3' 6'*	*F 3.5*	*100*	*OK*
3. Adam Crying	*3' 0'*	*F3.5*	*50*	*OK*
4. Adam and Sumana	*5' 0'*	*F 5.6 or 8*	*50*	*OK*
5. Adam in Bath	*3' 6'*	*F 8.6*	*50*	*OK*

Crossing Lake Toba

The East is a career.

Benjamin Disraeli

Kuta Diary

You get used to the charred vacant lot
no-one wants, Kuta's booze and burning,
the usual morning-after reek.
The awful indifference of its weather.

You walk from the beach
to the cenotaph's roll-call list.
Can't *not* read each and every name
the candles lit and those gone cold,
and you're skimming
before you go to manage the shoe factory.
But then you're back to walking, aimless,
among the holy orders,
their lives hand-carved
by the hundreds, into art and decoration,
where sex is cheap and *shopping* is an illusion
and 'Maya is the shop to be'.

Now, a little humbled
like a disrobed monk or a rich man
fretting on a no-fault divorce
dressed in rags, what difference
were you dreaming of a flute of airline champagne
smuggled off Air France or
a tumbler of bootleg Arrack, or whether,
blind with radiance, you had

another twenty years to live,
vowing to kill the guys who did this
and still keep a clean sheet on the moral front?

Sweet day of reckoning...
Until then teach beginner English,
practise at the rifle range,
and dance badly out of sync
with the high-caste girl next door.
Who among the angels would hear
if you crooned for her
and all God's creatures, from the rats on up?
Hibiscus festoons the dancers,
the dogs have nothing to fear,
the dance goes on, a little quicker
than before.

Nostalgia

First there were the bombs.
Then the Fall of Singapore,
and then its return.

Then there was the sundowner,
then the bullet point recipes
for WW2 American cocktails.

Then there were poolside romps
with vacationing English teachers,
sunburnished Nova Scotian girls

and behind them
a still life with Mexican palm
and a shelf of old Tequila bottles
backlit by a sunset
the colour of Angostura Bitters.

Then there was the Dubai go-between.
Then you went for the sainthood.

Then there were days of caramel brandy
and Bali Hai, beer of shabby Princes.
Then the cocktail windscreen wipers
and the spin-dry fluorescence
of a disco's ultra violet.

There was a driver parked by Heaven,
where makeshift futures men talked and stalked,
and chatted up the girls, the boys,
and the in-betweens.

Then there was the little guy
on Nowhere Corner
wired to HQ.

Then there was the secret code for laughter.
Then there was laughter.

For Effendy, Emperor of Icecream

Effendy, I like the way you avoid work. It is saintly.
You stay up late, endlessly smoking on your porch
listening to the owls.
When we turn back on the freeway, we take a detour,
find strong tea in a maligned part of town.
Someone driving past in a Cadillac
jolts a memory of flat plains and cafeterias:
Ahh Utah! Ahh little women of the prairies!
Back in the chai shop the light bulb factory
  workers gossip
and watch Tamil musicals on a giant Sony.
Lightning once struck
the skewer embedded in a Hindu's tongue.
Shall it do so once again?
But we are the virtuous and disconnected:
stroll about the kampong sucking toothpicks.
We made no ice-cream today you said,
with a look of triumph. Inshallah. Pray
for a sugar-led recovery; life so sweet
and sticky with discreet luxury.
We were never destined to make fighter jets.
Those yuppies need new flavours you said,
but I'm traditional. Tea is fine, or beer.
And home we went to 'Saving Private Ryan'
on your new DVD.

Nyepi

Grope around for matches.
Annual ritual blackout, island-wide,
ghosts get bored, start their engines & go
back to Java, Darwin, or another island.
Demand's inflationary
for séance & exorcism.
Part time waiters double as demons,
Barong & Leyak in cat-like form
roam the fishing village of no fish.
Unplug neon, blow out candles
in damp ten dollar rooms,
tell the traveller what's Royal or divine.
Books by torchlight? Forget it.
Everywhere PCs put to sleep.
When someone cleans the pool
someone collects the sheets, another
clips the hotel garden topiary.
When it's Nyepi they say
magicians disguise themselves as pigs
or glamorous women who kidnap street kids
& give them jobs.
They tell us: all this fuss ensures
the great darkness
is a darkness, the great abyss
exists & why ghosts
are fooled by this. The party

lights go out.
Then come on again, brighter!
The locals sigh immense relief
when the world is released

for what the morning brings
when someone cleans the pool,
someone collects the sheets, another
clips the garden topiary.

The Curse of the Chicken Rice Hawker, Penang

You discover they lie
those siblings in the mother country, those parasites
who spend each hard-earned cent of your remittances
on Mao Tai and Fan Tan
and still beg for more –
when you see the opulent mansions of your cheating ancestors
and smell the simmering pots fill with your own cash
    and sweat
your never laying down the cleaver – well, you can imagine –

on their dog's paws a single piece of jade will turn black
    with the years.
You pay off the mortgages on their graves
and yours will be dug in the slagheap of mines –
    well, you can imagine.

How a singular duty has led you to this –
your shop full of dragons in a year of crying tigers.
You say: 'This is my wealth, my friend, a secret duck
    sauce for two dollars.
But when I think of our ancestors – ahh you can imagine –
worse than the bloody government!'

The burning of their boats shall commence!
the ripping of photos,
the forgetting of their names!

The Inheritance

My friends were fishing when I left for Ambarita
to pursue my inheritance
in its seedy backblocks.

I return to a shanty cataract oozing
over the volcano's eye.
I am lucky they say:

no more do they smoke the heads of enemies.
Locals say there are no heads left
to rival the dollars of agents – pronounced 'angels' –

from spirit empires far away.
Ancient home-grown monsters
sour-fleshed, go unbaptised

to measureless depths. Banished.
But the ghost blue mascot
named the Nila fish

continues to spawn, endemic, bony but edible,
while across the mountain a rumoured wilderness
    of gold
buys out innocence.

Laundry girls arrived in town with 'cannibal' dowries.
Rumour made the rounds, how
the head priest's mistress drowned her grief

in a bottomless well. Her secret baby
had his hazel eyes –
a vision of sapphires and silver, inlaid and overwrought.

Perhaps the white Father was a fake – his touch
had limited powers, hurting then healing, bending
   our bodies
to his will.

When the Empire collapsed he left us to our
   wounds and mourning,
a crowd grieving on the shore
cascading tears, a Sunday fugue of wailing.

We watched the fathers go,
their absence re-enacted in processions
in a spray of chintz, free cigarettes and holy water.

With my departure I abandoned soothing black magic
and learned new hymns I modified
for prison conditions and three string guitar.

Too old for lullabies
I welcome my newfound old friends, the fishermen.
Happy to be caught I take deep breaths

and bite down hard on the silver hook
hidden like a language in their lures.
Who had given it such strange attraction, that hook,
the word?

She? The goddess of the lake?
All the beautiful waters of this world
she dragged me through. Nearly drowning

to prove my love.
Was it heaven? What the fathers had dismembered
we had suffered making one again.

The lake gave and took, and gave.
'Be modern: escape poverty!' she urged delirious
with hope
that day of proclamation.

I left that time for the city where they say
a million hooks will end your dream
and everyone sells you a gift.

The Bargain

They bargain & agree: the child & elder
scour the marketplace

for tart fruit that's hard to peel
but irresistible three days after picking.

Grannie turned the pawnshop inside-out
trading rubies for rations: some blue-grey duck eggs,

a wad of betel nut, or half a dried fish.
Gambler since the 20s, she outlived a rubber boom

three military coups, three Kings,
and countless warlords driven to modernise.

She never could cover her breasts for
propaganda edicts, or wear a hat.

She peeled fruit, basketfuls
for both of them. The kid combine-harvested

the never-empty tray. His graduate mother
her blue-eyed husband

were tall mythic gods printing cash.
So fashionable, what do they get up to?

Time-ravished, leathery and dentureless
she crooned for the heat-rashed brat,

Tiger Balmed his temples, fanned
the velvet of his skin

banker to her greedy client
his mouth an avid conduit.

Asthma, nine children and her
faithless spouse prayed too much, Grandma's

bargain allowed for bribe and chiding
so the plate shone clean.

The child in his childishness knew
experience, and sensed the limit of her body

as he climbed into her lap, exhausted,
a little bloated animal.

His selfish pleasure pulled her limb from limb,
but what dissolved her jaw and gums

were pink alkaloids of a crushed nut
wrapped in a bittergreen leaf.

Craving's law no-one broke when a storm
could brew air too thick to breathe,

the place her body would go:
pregnant clouds, cataracts of midday glare –

milky, churned, dark, like nothing
he understood.

Translations From the Malay, 1930.

Lesson 28: kena, to get or incur

The prau met with a stiff breeze yesterday. These steps were broken, but I knew not why. For some reason I had lost my job, but the writing room gets the afternoon sun, and the brushes get wet with rain. My white shirt is ink stained, the arm of my coat is dirty with whitewash, my trousers are splashed with mud. I live in a house of wood that has been painted, and it will last for a long time. I got Abdul to fetch two tins of kerosene and Baba had to pay the broker two dollars commission. The cook complained that her knife was rust eaten. Get rid of it with powder I said. Nonya had yet to return for her mother was ill.

Lesson 29: Adverbs

I had heard enough. What else was there for the gardener had swept almost everything. Eat some more, speak less, give the child more pudding, I urged Baba to speak a little more quietly around the guests. The driver wanted more wages, but how much more, he could not say. Really! He is not one to describe things precisely, as he lives in a world simply. The Sundanese maid is exceedingly pretty, exceedingly. The cook's sauces are very delicious. So if you wait awhile I will read all the letters. Please don't think I am an idiot, James, well not completely. I sold the Humber for 100 pounds too little. By the end of the month I shall be much better. The Padre drinks far too much, but what's the harm in asking for a little more?

Lesson 30: Verb: boleh, to be able

Are you able to eat curry, Major? Or sambal? I can manage it but Cook's never been able to understand that we Europeans can't take too many chillies. I believe you will be able to digest those kinds of vegetables. I usually eat cabbage in the morning and cauliflower in the evening. Cook's wife has learned to make ice kajang. Delicious, if the teeth can take all that syrup. A cigar? Yes, Driver might be able to take you to the godown. Can you come tomorrow night, Boy? We need an extra hand. (Really, Major, what can you do: if a boy's no good, it can't be helped.) Not much I can do to stop the milk going sour.

Lesson 41: Verb: jadi, to become

You must become a witness in this case, how the sultan went to fat. At least Bun Keng's been promoted to master of the Hokkien School. It was fortunate for us that we didn't happen to go on leave to Kota Baru. What would have become of Baba? Worse Luck! The rain did not come and the wind rose. We wait in hope for the day when tapioca will be cheap. We almost went mad when the bangsal caught fire. Sometimes, I despair, that Boy will never come to anything!

Revision

What do you want to buy? A cartload of lime?

Go to the bank first and return by tram.

He seldom shoots of an afternoon.

How do you hope to be clever, Hashim, being always asleep?

Perhaps the padre will not return to dine this evening.

My, what a fool. He just does not know how to perform Boys Work!

It has been quite a while since he worked in a sawmill.

I believe all the same he is innocent.

Cairns

Two hours off the plane from Sydney;
    and my mother and I, poolside
        where Mimosa meets Palm

have hit the red burgundy, and talk
    of fixing the condo, and why she's here,
    living out retirement
        in a cycle of sugarcane harvests.

The streaky rain is intermittent,
    the south's blowing in, fronting up to a sticky north
        of pink tinged cumulus,

warm trade winds, the killer jellyfish,
    the sandflies. We talk of
        why the Riverland casks go off on road trains
        heading north

and why the shopping malls are freezing.
    Only four hours by plane
        to Bangkok, and the tropical fruit's better.

We talk of how she'd come here – not for the 'culture',
    (just ask the Japanese:
        did you come here

for the culture? They turn away, assiduously
polite, utterly perplexed).
No, there're better reasons than the culture.

'Thai kick boxing is very popular here.'
No fan of violence she opens
the local *Holloway News*:

Dylan 'Hatchet' Hayworth is defending
his North Queensland title.
Di Quirk, her 'grey power' neighbour

will tell you how happy she was
to win Maddy the Lioness Bear at
Edmonton's Trivia Quiz.

At the Festival of the Knob, Heinz (my mother's man)
tells me the Festival founder
had been 'a *beche de mer* fisherman

from Yorkshire'.
I think he meant a Yorkshireman
who's become a *beche de mer* fisherman.

Though who knows with Heinz, whose
word for culture is '*Kultur*', and for whom
Hegel is light reading.

In Cairns anything's possible.
'The sun cures all confusion!' she says,
as she polishes her bifocals.

It's good then, I suppose,
to be a war veteran in Cairns, or
a veteran's young Asian wife.

Numerous functions at the RSL, e.g.
Filipino smorgasbord on Sundays
(a week's work of stewed pork and sweet yam).

There's Toastmasters, a 50 and Over group,
a Shirley Club (all Shirleys welcome),
a Garden club, two or three Arthritis
Sufferers groups,

a Single Parents group,
a Lefties group and a Soul Foods group
who get together at the Marlin Coast
Neighbourhood Centre,

who quote all major religions
and listen to rainforest music.
Not that my Mum would want to belong

to any of them. 'Too déclassé',
she sniffs,
'like bush mangoes!'

There're her neighbours, the Holloway Europeans:
Charlene, for example,
barefoot, tall, fungal,

skinny Charlene from Dapto,
who lived on the Hippie trail in the 60s,
smoked hash in Afghanistan,

hung out in Amsterdam, sailed the French Pacific
with Marcel the 'bricoleur' from Noumea.
Marcel the Kombi man, who'll fix anything

for the price of a beer.
'Moving here, have you changed?' I ask.
'Have you?' she replies, scoffing.

'Much else has. They say Cairns is booming:
more bribes, more deals,
more backyard chook sheds concreted over.'

Not listening, she sails on her own
    winedark sea of local gossip:
        'The problem is the French: they avoid tax,

only think of themselves.
    Who cares if Marcel was union rep
        for Renault, or organised the barricades?'

My mother says that Charlene
    once camped in Pat Pong Road,
        hung out with Thai men,

then denied she wanted the sex.
    Mother said that Charlene said:
        'But no sex. Give me drinks, food, the odd pash, OK,

but no sex.'
    But when Charlene confirms it
        next day at the beach barbie

I know it's true. ('Is that true,' I ask?
    'Sure, sure it's true,' Charlene replies.)

———

The next day mother debriefs:

'And you know
        Charlene and the French,
                they think I am

inferior, helpless Asian housewife!
        Racists, ALL racists,
                especially Q, from Vanuatu,

and he's half black, Kanak!
        Social Security, they can't get enough of it.
                Charlene speaks to me in *pidgin*. Imagine.

Is it Dutch? New Guinea? I can't give a fuck!
        French, they can only talk to each other
                                                        in *French*!
Heinz gets so bored.
        Good thing Heinz is out fishing.
                Once he starts. Especially when they

talk about the War, making
        SS jokes.' (But we never did?)
                'The French, that's the problem. They complain

about Japanese,
        JP (best French chef in Port Douglas) says
                'Japanese are tough bosses.'

OK. Have to be.
They're Japanese, what you expect?

I lend them literature – like Patrick White,
Conrad, *Islam in the Soviet Union…*
Next day returned. Not read!'

(Pause, opening
of new cask. Taste test, then
topping up of wine glasses.)

She continues: 'At least Madame Petite (Madame Mini)
knows what living means:
a sit down lunch, eat.

Civilised. They have a beautiful garden,
à la Provençal… they let me pick their chillies.'
'Now *that's* culture,' I say.

'JP loves Thai food…
They think I don't understand
what it means to be European.

They call me "Chinee cook". I lived in London
fucking four years.
Bloody!'

'What about the Aussies?' I ask.
'What about the Dewslips across the road?'
'They're very kind, they help me take out

the recycling bin sometimes.
John helps Heinz with the boat.'
'What about Kiwi?'

'Heinz likes Kiwi. Kiwi makes home brew.
Kiwi's from New Zealand.'
'What about Oscar Von Seca?'

(From Bondi Beach he drops in
once a year for a curry and
checks on rental investments.

No-gluten diet and jungle jogging twenty klicks a day,
Oscar the retired weightlifter and ex-journalist
who'd been sacked by Murdoch.)

'Oh Oscar drops by. He's got Heinz investing
in margin loans for commercial property.
Just for pocket money, you understand.'

There's always Heinz, planning
to fly to Malaga and stay there four months.
Get away from the heat.

'I said, fine, do what you like. Why should I go here *there*,
    la-la-la, doing whatever HE likes?
        Last time in Madrid, we slept at the station!

I never go to Europe with him again.
    Europe – clapped out anyway.
        Nothing in Europe.

We're not lovers you know. Just friends now.
    Sex finished long time ago.
        I tell social security we're not *de facto*.

But now they put our assets together.'
    'No reason not to go,' I say. 'If you have the money.
        Have a holiday.'

'For the culture!' she says.
    'For culture and what's left of it!' I say.
        And we're halfway there, as I

go to cleaning the pool, and the Osaka
    Express roars in
        on the final approach.

Cambodian Poems

Positive and negative impulses exist within us all.
Those of us who shine brightest are not those who have no darker side,
but those who are fully aware of their negativity,
who keep their darkness in check by increasing their light.
Taro Gold

Travels in Indo-china.
Etc.
Henri Mouhot

A Map of Cambodia

after Yao Feng's 'Map of China'

Does anyone out here deserve thanks
for the map?
Magenta for bombed areas,
beaches named after hotels
islands sold off to foreigners.
Note the stippled effect of forced evictions.
Shaded areas mean gas.
One piece for the Thais,
another for the Viets and BHP.
The plantations, rubber
and what else?
Golf courses even generals can't afford.

As Home-boy Prach
might sez
Take some California in return
rap it out
and call yourself a new American
sell some crack
tag the neighbourhood
and get shipped back.

Still, the lotus ponds too numerous to count.
Where the sugar palms are
you'll find a Cambodian.

A river flowing backwards
when you need it.
Under one map there's another
rising on the tide
as the pain recedes.

Ruins

In Phnom Penh a mountain of junked bicycles
is a monument to Welcome!
but Siem Reap's giant preying mantis
toting an AK-47
at the Foreign Correspondents Club
counts as art.

What's your particular
welding fantasy?
Will the future of man
speak English, sufficient
to order cocktails?

Fairy lit, aromatic and red
we've hired a ten-armed Apsara
to squeeze our tired feet
in a sushi barn
with touch-screen translation
draught Sake
and a drop-down menu
where the frog legs still quiver.

They had a gun buy-back too
and a five year plan
yet to run its course
after which

cash will be king
no questions asked
no feedback required

Onwards then
to Sihanoukville's
Siberian tropical resort
famous for giant catfish,

our 'high net worth weekend'
that 'starts from a low base'
as they say on CNN.

Expect a daily interruption
or 'macro-slowdown'
ending in catastrophic
loss of reception.

Expect a shipment from China
of pink motorbikes and
the latest pumps.

Essentials: words and phrases

How much does it cost?
or
I'd like to give this to you

It took no time at all to learn what I needed
and years to realise what I'd learned
was what I didn't need.

What's more important
the classifier of clouds
or the clouds, the scrap collector
or the scrap?

Like your poem, Jane, about a list
of no use to business:

delicate, wrist, telescope
relic, telepathy

Reliable and *narcotic* I'd keep

so too *reap*, *harvest* and *yield*
for the agricultural economy.

As there is
for long things, round things,

flat things, and even
things made out of glass

as yet no classifier
for things
no-one wants,
or
for the collector:

the bottles a boy sorts
more valuable than the boy.

Postcards (after Michelle Cahill)

Siem Reap Dawn

Traffic noise – there isn't much
the road's a washed out laterite
and the smell is fish – the drying kind.
Nothing spinning
but the *moto* driver's hungover head.
Light breaks through – clean white clouds
and the girls are busy sweeping.
Foreigners dressed in tomb raider hats,
French and nervous,
sparrows peck at monuments.

TV going off and on
I sip beer with the Russians
the rodents have all been eaten.
And Buddha, hung with fairy lights
visibly delighted
withdraws some cash from an ATM.

Forest Wat, Cambodia

Who knows if suffering's inquiry leads you anywhere
but back to suffering? Yes, there are no rainbows
shining at the end of the runway
but the craving to fall asleep
before the train arrives at the station
is an idea of grace, temporary, essential.
The tracks were ripped out years ago
by lads who knew more about suffering
than we ever will. No end to it.
And yet, you're right Michelle, the children
still wave here, though hardly a soul over forty,
and those who remember can't quite recall
the historic meaning of their lives, or
how their names are spelt: just
to have come this far, along the road,
just this sack of green leaves, this hammock in the trees.

The War Never Ends

A woman sheltering under a rattan mat
from a thunderous downdraft of Hueys
by the banks of the Mekong;
her last recollection of home.

Your story won't translate
if no-one can read the cards
or can recall
the exact sound of an RPG-7
hitting a storehouse of rice.

Who here would want to?
Books like those
sell better in the States,
but here

temple bells and roosters
will always wake you
from your dream,
sounding just when the poem
needs them.

Cut! the bells say, Silence!
In that jump-cut montage
of heroes fanning out
to secure the poem's perimeter

threatened now
by an influx of Gangsta Rap.
Foreigners will fall for you
when you tease them
about their size, their impatience,
their fake ragged clothes,

the way they say they care for you
in that sunset of least resistance.
How about that happy ending
he signed for at the front desk?
Is it still available?
I want to help, they say
in a dream they had of coming back.

Dukkha (Craving)

It came as a surprise, most of all to me,
to have come this close
to a thug's approach
to ritual sacrifice.
All hot breath, and a scratch
that might've been my last
so deep and deep enough
to separate forever
my mind from my throat.
Not what I expected
and once I was gone
what man left would defend
my bones from a scavenging pariah?

Put all this down
to karma, my excessive love
of champagne, steak, ghazals, hashish –
in *this* life I walked through
like a Prince of arcades,
blindly unafraid
through the streets –
not life previous

which was even more
stunningly decked out

in luxury without end,
paid for,
debt free –
or so I had thought.

Songkhran, Siem Reap River

On the banks of the river
we would be wet, if the water ran,
and the children could afford a bucket.
Even the frisky cows know
staying dry is staying alive.
Here, cows know more about road safety
than townsfolk selling photocopied
books on genocide.
The tour guides 'make English work for them'
on a hill of wild mint and gravel.
As for fire and ash, even that's preserved
and the fish are best when smoked.

So much to celebrate, and lives are short.
Chasing snakes or frogs
harvesting morning glory
in the Raffles Hotel gardens.
What I wish for is a place
to park my bike, a table
to write on, some roses,
a waterfall, a quiet
bench on the river: this place to read
and imagine the parents I never knew.
Something, maybe my soul, floats
like a hyacinth downstream,

to be netted, collected for feed,
or caught, like a sandal that's
lost its foot, snagged in an outburst
of pandanus.

Songkhran, Bangkok

The whores are drunk and soaked to the skin,
their cell phones packed in Ziploc bags.
You pick the one with the platinum specs,
the uni student look-alike.
You respect literacy, if it sells.
You want to do it while she's reading.
Number one best lover, you want her to say;
instead it's: 'Shoot me with your water pistol'.
Sacked by the bank, Dad went AWOL,
the kid needed feeding back in the village.
Sex pays better than data entry
and your new office mates less bitchy.
A choice between the gutter
and this place. No stars.
Another drink? she asks. You like lady, or butterfly?
I'm Cambodian, crossed with something else, canine perhaps.
You lie! she says, but true! you say,
how a man a lot like that can sell his kids,
on special days like this, load them
onto pickup trucks
and head for the border.
Every day, every night,
rooms blazing, full of handicams.
All of this for a new pulp thriller
with gold embossed title
and your author shot in green fatigues.

Aubade I

Wake up to hammering, a retching child
and Khmers getting married
with the official
Wedding Music Compilation
on a 72-hour loop and full volume PA.
To them silence is Hell.
A certain medication
will cure the child and
all your life will fit together.
One pill equals the average monthly salary.
Harmonious as a buzzsaw.
On the clef above
more sparrows and cockcrow,
bass drum and xylophones.
The maid drags the laundry into the sun,
the child is racked in spasm.
Or is it the neighbours
de-sexing the puppy
with a kitchen knife?
It's the underworld again, rumbling.
Temple thieves stand ready
to chisel out a dancer's face.
I reach out for the pills, shaking
with a fragile compassion. I mean
drink them down and nothing stays down
on mornings like this,

no doctor on my mobile.
Last night a hotel laser show blinded the hospital,
then it rained, thanks to Indra,
and it was possible
to keep reading in the dark.

A Note on the River

a river's there
for cutting grass

for police to
drop their pants

have their fill
al fresco

for girls to sober up

on a life
wittled away

by extortion

icons of shame
drifting in the garden shadows

who complains?
no-one

no-one
writes or can

this my accident
of passing by

Silk: A Wearer's Guide

A scruffy boy, I kept them in a box, and learned
to watch them fatten on a forest floor of green mulberry
and spin themselves to a timetable.
I'd wear silk in war and watch bullets bounce off my chest.
Or, as head of state at an APEC conference,
line up for a photo-shoot in garish silk pyjamas.
I'd burn silk to alleviate a bleeding nose,
or, constipated, eat it with a dollop of syrup.
I imagine my mother married
in a discarded D-Day parachute, though in truth
three months pregnant she wore Chanel, white raw silk.
Nothing could be cooler in a London May.
If anything, silkworms made China.
No silk, no Madame Butterfly boudoirs, peachy and pink,
no po-co allegory, no going-away gift of ties.
Pol Pot had looms burnt, the weavers thrown to dogs,
demoted to spinning peasant cotton.
Because Gandhi (the people's choice?) chose muslin.
I too would have perished, like all worms,
had I spoken the secret lingo of weavers.
Two threads of fibroin or brins glued together in sericin
make a bave. Unable or unwilling to confess
a plain English equivalent, did they deserve death
in black Dacron fatigues?
Four hundred metre lengths of spun figure-of-eights,
and no worm can turn. Boiled in grege, raw or reeled,

the thicker thread for weft, the finer thread for warp.
The unspooling well-wrought worm makes a tasty
deep fried snack;
the lesser formed make chicken feed.
Now that even children know how silkworms live, recycled
for profit and a beauty nature never intended,
who wants to be an ugly moth?
I was a weaver addicted to that code,
reincarnated, returning to the guild,
then *rehabilitated*, as the Maoists used to say.
Prior to the dyeing process, if the ashes of a kapok tree
can't be found, soap will bleach the skeins.
For dyes the best are barks, roots,
rhizome, seeds and leaves of an old Khmer forest
de-mined to a 99 percent ISO rating.
Tinctorial plants shimmer in the eye.
Nature's madder red refracts blue, then green
(as if spot-lit in a TV studio set) then yellow.
The dealers know what yields indigo, what
doubles as a pesticide, disinfects a cut
or stuns the fish more cheaply than grenades.
From indigo leaf derives indican, hence conversion
by alkaloid
to indoxyl. Alum and green vitriol are mordants;
with green Sappan wood the mix turns red and purple.
The cow hoof tree I've never seen, while iron,
especially military ordnance (like a tank rusting in
a mangrove)

is abundant as rain. Jackfruit, domestic and wild
gives saffron; for a deeper brown, add
ebony berries or turmeric; cassia yields you beige.
For red, the excreta of the sap-sucking lac bug
never fails, and the old rivals Science and Art
break down, fermenting in a vat of silk.
Natural green – now rare – makes way
for what's in vogue today: overdyes of mango bark yellow
spliced with indigo, which is *fugitive*, as they say
   in the trade:
Wednesday's colour becomes with time and washing
the colour of another day, Monday.
This has consequences:
the confused mnemonics of school children,
the disconnect of colours with calendars;
the rhyme I used to chant, fading in my room of worms.

Coins Falling

after Agnes Lam's 'Coins Falling'

Dear Agnes

How I wanted to respond
to your poem 'coins falling'
but here there are no coins
and no buses
that will take me where I want to go.

And if you'd been around
in the seventies
there was no money anyway
nor places to go
just a lot of wailing
and people cooking dogs

no stop
for pork and beef
or fish and eggs

but the crabs would come
to eat the dead on the river

and if you'd stopped for your
harmonica
you were wise to bury it

for a future time
to use in heaven

and when the guests left
they had no pictures to show
or almond biscuits

there were sounds
to remember

like money falling
into a beggar's bowl

but no poems to write
and end like that.

Shiva, Uma, Ravanna

She clings to him like a breasted baby.
The palace is shaking. The whole mountain
off-limits to riffraff. He can crush the lot of them,
helpers and sages included. Some days
the intrigue is irritating: Ravanna, jealous demon
shatters the calm
with a call to arms (ten arms and four faces).
Tigers jump away, as if a train
were coming to run them down.
Horseface keeps on meditating.
Do something, Uma wails, my beautiful hair will unfurl
and the forest will crumble like a tower.
Perhaps the solution is a rain of fire
or a cloud festooned in flashing lights.
Hit the demon on the head: it shatters.
On the turntable of the heavens Shiva
extends a big right toe, and pushes.
Uma passes the test, flexes in fear, petrified.

Aubade 2

Now I have been to China.
No more breaking 'the insteps
of wellborn Chinese girls'
to decorate escape memoirs.
Just a bang on the door at 6.
It's the party secretary's secretary
making sure I won't
miss the tour bus.

I would like to wake at daybreak
in a highrise on the sea.
In fact, there I would write more

at that hour, oh, of the dark suited men
smoking in the car park
and at the tomb of Confucius,
puffing on Double Happiness
among a thousand burial mounds.

Filial duty is a little boy
collecting coke cans for his Dad,
and for that he received
a Double Happiness.

I would like to write more of the woman
who sold giant turnips of green skin

and purple flesh, which pucker your lips
with their pepper. I would like to write more
with their pepper and without
stealing your lines,
the ones that reek at morning's coolest
hour of day.

I wake in old 'Funan'.
It was clear to Zhou Da Guan (1296) why
the Khmers never travel at night.
They prefer to wake
at the earliest, and gather their nets, uproot
weeds at dawn, then resume
the chiselling of the frieze.
But they have no need
to write of waking, as far as I know.
There are no portraits of waking, none
of sleeping in the afternoon in empty
second hand bookstores.
But still they sleep as the world wakes.
It is a gift, to wake then, in old Funan,
to find oneself in thought.

S21

Of what will they dream?
Which song will they remember? What name
will they want to name – the bones – in their darkness?
Mario Licón Cabrera, *Osario*

The way – ideally – we might remember:
a glass case or a neat Perspex tower
of skulls and thighbones.
Blood and rust melded together
in the springs of an old French style bed base.
An old cartridge case shit can.
Samplers of jumbled DNA,
a room of ragged cast-offs.
How to come away from it,
to photograph it, how long to stay there and stare
at the spattered tiles and the ripped out wiring.
To wonder what endless days
reading an archive of ten thousand 'confessions'
does for the eyes; I'm sick of questions
no-one wants to answer.
A forensic display of bullet wound trauma,
all logic and angles
is somehow a relief.

In the schoolyard recanters stacked up
end on end, queued for each device, machines
no theory committee

could calibrate to perfection.
Lies, half-truths, false leads, endless plot.
To write 'my life is not worth a bullet'
concludes more than narrative.
How to sign off a letter
with terror's salutations – and after that?
'Ahhrgh' perhaps, or a dog's whimper,
or a dragging chain.
Someone who'd been to Belsen
had written 'Justice' in the visitor's book.
But this was a rustic and ham-fisted machine
with no industrial prototype.

I too have to write, wondering where I am
on the chain-link of paranoia
connecting a tyrant to a farmer's son
who was handy with a shovel;
someone like the accountant across the corridor
doing the company's credit/debit sheet –
the guy with *all* the stories, who
knew how to file, the one who said
he'd done his job protecting his nation
with a few blunt instruments
a fountain pen, and a beautiful signature.

The 32 Hells: A Sampler

For those condemned, judgment prologues pain.
Yama, whose province is time and death eternal,
sits on a buffalo, has many arms, and clubs,
and judges not, is merely executioner.
The higher being, the implacable, who points the club
    at you
and speaks of cruelties greatly diverse, without par.
    Godless minds by pain are sharpened
in great feats of imagination:
like a knife on a grindstone endlessly turning.

Thieves, indeed those who have stolen elephants,
sandals, parasols, or any kind of vehicle.
They will have their tongues pulled out
and demons shall stuff their mouths
with shredded feet and toss them into a raging sewer.
Those who shat in temples or defamed a guru
or seduced the wife of a high-born,
abortionists and charlatans,
have a dozen hells to choose.
The unjust will be chained and beaten,
then slashed by two-edged swords.
False witnesses shall be skinned and flayed alive
with a food grater, then hung from trees,
then ground down in a mortar.

Kidnappers will be plunged into a vat of molten lead.
The *hell of broken bones* is what it says.
Those who trampled the flowers in the gardens
and ponds and stole vegetables
will have stakes through their throats.
Adulterers and seducers of unmarried youth
shall be thrown to vultures and drowned in a lake of pus.
Licentious females will burn in a lake of marrow,
breasts hang flaccid as desiccated aubergines.
Fraudsters await a simmering cauldron of vermin.
Profane doubters, despisers of science.

So who can think a pit of worms is mild?
Greedy ones who have defamed the high-born
with their envy, prepare to have their jaws crushed
in a vice in the *hell of the oppressive mountain.*
Deforesters will hang head down among cactuses.
Flower-stealers shall have nails driven through their skulls
in the *hell of the lotus.*
Those who have eaten unconsecrated meat, await
the unspeakable, the hell of weeping.
In the *hell of thick darkness* they will be done with eyes
and wait in an eternity of queuing.

Exiles and debtors, let us say
hell is indeterminate and indecipherable.
What's to omit or overlook?

Everything they cannot name is here.
Those who speak on behalf
of their glorious organisation
think of everything.

The Triumph of Sangrama over the Traitor Kamvau

They begin with troubles in the East,
in the grey-zone foment and rebellion
among individuals of obscure origin,
the weedlike prevalence of usurpers.

They begin with scimitars, their glint,
the armoury that makes the sky shine.
Does one 'brandish' a pike or a lance?
Do they twang a bow in memory of their nerves?
The traitor, in a hurry, rushes forth
through a forest of sharp metal.

Before he sinks into the 'sleep of death'
the blood shall be described variously
as a flood, a gurgle, or a mountain range.
They are all blinded by an effulgence we
call our glory.

As the enemies advance
so comes a time to make eloquence of killing.
'Crazy man, Kamvau, I have long sought this moment.
Whoever attacks Indra is insane.
Are you not fearful?'

Once the proof of valour's laid upon the ground
it is time: 'Go to hell!' the rebels shout.
'And it's all one way!'
'Cease intimidation', the hero cries
and reaches for a magic arrow no fine words
deflect from its purpose.

Hostile arrows shall fall with such variety,
as a shower, or as a rain of flora
that land
with no ill effects on the general.
A secret form of feathered shaft
will bring down Kamvau, hence a list of entry points
where death shall enter:
head, heart, chest, jaw.

The soundtrack terrible,
regret sets in with the fallen remnants
grieving in the ruined chambers
of a stony heart, the rags of their certainty
ripped and fluttering in a malarial calm.

Dear Henri

Dear Henri

When you died your last fevered words
were incomprehensible to the servants.

These days it is not so easy
to discover anything,
or to re-discover anything,
let alone die looking.

I would like to begin my book,
To the Learned Societies of… etc.
I would like to be buried in Luang Prabang
where the chanting is atrocious.

I would travel, trusting to Providence,
with a case of Bordeaux, Cognac, sardines,
and a King Charles cocker spaniel.

I would like to be writing in my jungle tent,
only to be interrupted
by the unexpected visit of a governor
offering a Rhinoceros hunt
in my honour.

The dream never came to pass:
that great cotton plantation
on the shores of the Tonle Sap
(priced in francs)
intended to surpass the Americas
then in Civil War –
a nation eating itself
like this place has done for centuries.

You gained nothing by the excursion
but the pleasure of having been
a chronicler of the habits of a curious people,
intended to gratify a public
with a taste for amazons
and ruins built by giants,
for savage but kindly people.
One could civilise them,
though you knew one wouldn't.
'All sensibilities seem deadened among them,
proud and great cheats' said the Abbe
of the Annamites.

Your subjects were lively but obstinate,
generous but vindictive,
intelligent but dissembling,

slow to get into a passion,
but terrible when they did so.
Their food stank
but diversity of taste
was laudable.
How they weakened with dysentery
but still looked cheerful.

Depressed by the monotony and driven mad
by the torment of insects, you considered
your exquisite options: what to admire most
in an elephant flicking sand flies
off its back with a branch –
the sensitivity of its skin,
its patience,
or its intelligence?

A town could be stifling
unable to waken your sympathies
with its *too great a number of humans*.

Our aim? To counsel, soften, enlighten
and convert with a gift.

I appreciate you telling me
how you were cured of Athletes Foot
due to your scrupulous cleanliness
and that the inhabitants of the jungles

learned the range of your rifle
and the calibre of your balls.

I would like to be travelling
with gifts,
a pair of tortoiseshell spectacles,
a bottle of scent, a sedative mixture
for a chief with rheumatism,
a button or a cigarette
for the still suckling child.

I would like to be surrounded
by superstition, ghosts, spirits and demons,
and not believe in any of it.

Now we will know how the hunter
was once truly beautiful,
how, on hearing a creature
gliding through the canopy,
you reached for your gun.
We will know
how to shoot a leopard
through the heart,
how it prowls thick undergrowth,
before it hears the report of your gun,
as it leaps, wounded mortally
then drops, the creature extended
lifeless.

At your feet.
It is beyond
description, for
whatever is profound
is indescribable
and writing is an exercise
with invisible ink, like
a patchwork of moonlight in the foliage:
Phrai stood with a sabre in one hand
and a torch in the other, pursuing
the fishes in the stream.

Let's be modest, your notes were
hasty, rough, with no claim to any merit
but to record the truth.
Destined as good books are
to see the light.

I would like it if
someone regretted
I had been French.

I would be grateful
if someone named a beetle
even a minor one,
after me.

Louis De Carne's Diary

Stunned by the noise of the waters we reached Khemarat
where M. Delaporte awaited us.
Nothing could express the horror
of the petty mandarins, the imbecile governor,
the yellow waters twisting through a narrow pass,
a child of seven smoking a cheroot,
or the site of a prisoner impaled by the tusks
of an elephant.
The light a deadly shade, the forest a blacker hue of
green,
the boat shaped serpent-like, whirlpools we could not see.
The river all tributary – no-one knew or cared
for the source or predominant
direction of its flow, a river unfit
for commercial intercourse.

Man had fled its banks, an abyss on both sides.
I was hot, too hot after my ramble
through an expanse of fetid mud.
But I could write all night in my tent
cobwebbed in ennui and
sucking on the leg bone of an iguana,
or recline under the implacable serenity of the heavens,
the all-powerful constraints
of influences so fatal to human personality
that thought dies away by degrees

like a flame in a vacuum.
At least I knew there were guards
(of vagabond stock, with the timid air of the aborigine)
whom I barely trusted
posted around the perimeter.

Francais

We talked about brochures
for the elite catering school –
the number of permissible fonts,
what the Cambodians like
what Westerners don't.

The curious blurred line in
a master-slave relationship,

the curious intersection
of semiotics
and tribal *nepotisme*,

how to be a player,
faire savoir versus
savoir faire,
my out-of-date
guide book
so useless…

Theories of the post-
colonial, politics, blogs,
pro-this, anti-that…

All too abstract now
once I'd seen

the afterlife glow
of the exhaust pipe blister
on her perfect calf
and watched entranced
her expert
application of Elizabeth Arden,

the arabesques
of her eyebrows
reflected in the rearview mirror.

Only two weeks in the country!

The way she accelerated
le moto
and disappeared down the track
and from behind
looked just like a local,

with an implacable gloss
heading for a crêperie
on Sivatha Boulevard
to meet a creep
who'd want to spike her drink.

Maybe, in six months,
she might eat anything, even spiders,

go crazy like Gauguin,
learn to paint in the dark,

and in six years
live on her wits
on borrowed dope, money and time,

not ever knowing
when it's time to leave

or how to say so
like the locals do.

Aubade 3

And what of waking
in the afternoon, after a dream of
nights when jackals stalk the oasis?
In the absence of a revolution
where does the mind go in siesta?
That feeling
of having missed a century
in a blink of an eye,
as you wake with the sun going down.
It was like this
for the French at Dien Bien Phu in 1954.
And before they could ask meaningful questions,
Bang! It was all over!

Meanwhile the palace slept, another novice
escaped into poverty and fame.

It's the same
dozing off in the waiting room
as the bamboo train disappears for good
into the hills of white elephants.
It's too easy, this drifting off
like Martin Sheen on R and R.
He saw the horror, checked his eyebrows in the mirror,
then smashed up the hotel.
You go AWOL on any excuse:

to rest your eyes
or ease a minor back ache.
Was it the cow you photographed
that morning, the queues
at the dengue hospital?
Does this count as a metaphor for love,
or a kind of neglect by design, the body's
failing to sleep and wake
at the proper time?
It can't be jetlag or the ghost
of Confucius haunting
the Chinese Garden in Qufu.
The day's sounds too busy, like child's play
or finches roosting in the eaves,
the neighbours gossiping as you wake,
counting money and dressing children.
The heat you didn't reason with
or calculate, the fan on full blast.
There are poets you know
who hardly sleep.
Your method is different.
You wake with a guilt hangover and
a mangrove for a face
after three coffees made in Vietnam.
No doubt the maid had drugged you.
All this money and nothing to do

in a world where capital never sleeps.
To be expected from an old dog, not you.
Tonight you'll pay, sleepless in Seattle
or Singapore, too alert, too aware
as the silences close in.

For the River and the Spring Again

after Meng Jiao

Over the river
lotus and pandanus simmer

in rain lies the late monsoon
verdant, burgeoning

there is no honest exile
I can go home anytime

after the rain
children sing

the world's near corners
hunched over a card game

money changes hands
to show the first light's welcome

the river comes silent
lapping the banks
where the frogs won't shut up

what water here compares
to the Kingly dust of Roluos?

what is spring:

the boat that takes you nowhere
the cart upturned in mud?

take me he would
could I shift him from slumber

my one clean dollar
I'll offer.

Morning Protocol

Money is a kind of poetry
Wallace Stevens

It was time for breakfast
but there was no breakfast.

The statues had been waiting
too long for their morning's

offering of flowers, sweet water.
Gorgeous flower vendors

making beds and cleaning
the five star toilets.

No shortage of offerings.
Luxuriance. But

always the hunger,
the empty shelf

where the flowers
should go.

If not flowers, then rice,
cigarettes, an orange.

What warning was there in this?

Who had spoken,
who had heard?

True, the neighbours
whispered: he didn't believe,

he would do away
with all statues.

But he believed in the tray,
and a big tip he threw

with great fuss and ceremony
on a battered tray of nothing.

Aubade 4

Love? Are there metaphors
we haven't mentioned?
We are surrounded
by minutes and hours
we can never use.
The romance of our huge uselessness
begins in a fake Versailles garden
dotted with Hindu deities.
All that time that will
always be ours.
Then there are
multiple awakenings
consecutive rebirthings,
practice runs for
the final time.
The day chimes – it says
move towards me.
Be present
when it matters,
shift consciousness
to a purely horizontal
position.
Each version of ourselves
more polished and sincere
than the one before;
less alert, less awake
than the one to come.

Swimming Pool

Stop time now. Romanesque, or Khmer
no-one can decide. No need to decide.

I was seriously thinking (like expats do)
of getting a dog, for company.

Some sort of pedigree to suit
my particular physique.
A bulldog, a boxer, something flattering.

Here, the pathos of the wealthy is palpable.
At least the water's real and up-to-date
and the tiles are a rich celadon green.

And all the water that there ever was
is the same water now.

Attendants flit around poolside
armed with grouting guns.

Should I suggest other improvements? I should not.

In the gym the very white girl's got her trainers on,
does a DVD worth of pilates (morse code with legs).

If anything's desired everywhere
it's 'a strong abdominal core'.

The Chinese princess snaps herself
like the catwalk model in a Nokia ad.
Big white teeth gleaming in the sun
doing ballet steps with a life preserver.

Her fiancé smokes and swims and…smokes.

My wife pops another Gastrolite
and reads *What's On in Phnom Penh*.

I have surrendered on letter number 4 of an ancient
    alphabet
so curly, designed by priests to defeat mass literacy.

I'm reading *The Philosopher's Dog*
by Raymond Gaita. How lucky they are,
even the dumbest mutts, to be alive and loved,
who know so much more about us
than we do.

Poem

The basket can never conceal the elephant indefinitely
Barking dogs seldom bite
Words are weapons
Roses have thorns, love has obstacles.

Real gold is not afraid of the fire
The basket can never conceal the elephant indefinitely
Barking dogs seldom bite
Words are weapons.

Revolutionaries must be pulled from the earth like diamonds
Real gold is not afraid of the fire
The basket can never conceal the elephant indefinitely
Barking dogs seldom bite.

Little by little, the bottle will fill
Revolutionaries must be pulled from the earth like diamonds
Real gold is not afraid of the fire
The basket can never conceal the elephant indefinitely.

Leaves fall off not far from the trunk
Little by little, the bottle will fill
Revolutionaries must be pulled from the earth like diamonds
Real gold is not afraid of the fire.

Aubade 5

Bishma on a bed of arrows

I, Prince of Darkness,
wake on a cushion of arrows.
A bed for a warrior,
so it was said
by the enemies
who shot them.

Nobody tells me
when to die.

In the heat of the melee
who could tell
friend from foe?
No matter, they
    suspend me
    for the next thousand years
above a stone cold floor
of congealed tears.
This means
I am a good loser,
a man who's great
but not quite great enough.

The Scream

A child wailing in the river naked,
as if planted, all torso
and nothing else
in a canal of litter.
One eye covered with a thong,
an insane frozen salute.
Two kids stand watch,
though it seems they aren't the final terror.
Such wailing
demands a theory or a cause.
Had he lost something? His mind,
or his parents?
Did he have legs to scale
back up the bank?
Nobody knows and I can't know
if they care;
it's lunchtime
then siesta.
I have a bridge to cross.
Though we hesitate,
in recognition,
as if he's caught in a trap
and has my eye.
The child that's
fixed on the apparition;
and he wails again,

rooted to the riverbed,
as if his only pet
had drowned,
and its voice down there
was speaking, a puppy in the underworld,
or barking
much louder than the passing traffic
or the taunts of two bullies.
Maybe he had seen himself:
a watery exposure
slowly drowning.
As if the vision of two eyes
was too much, the mud
taking him down, sucking
at his limbs, the red river
draining his lungs of blood.

The Wearer of Amulets

An old boy soldier you meet by the river.
And you ask him
why he never died.
He won't struggle for an answer.

There was a time
when all he'd thought of
was a winning lottery stub

and another time
a bullet whizzed past,

a voice had whispered duck
which he did
and the bullet
hit his friend.

And the Law of Karma said
his friend deserved it
while he himself had not.

A few days previous
in a post-lunch lull in the fighting
he'd knelt, chanting, on a wooden board
balanced on a bell
the shape of Mount Meru, sacred mountain,

while the friend espoused
a dull malevolence, forever searched
for a curse upon enemies;
remained unwashed,
avoided temple grounds,
would never pass the image of Buddha.

His friend would have killed the fortune-teller
who predicted the waning of his power.

Today, when I ask him
why he didn't die
the old boy soldier says
he aimed his AK at the Viet
and never missed
and boasts of killing conscripts
younger than himself;
how he's tasted magic:
ivory, wild boar tusk
and the blended love philtre of oily liana,
dried python and the faeces
of a red vulture.

His friend who'd fallen
had worn a mother's milk-tooth amulet
a piece of gold of holy repute

round his neck –
a cheaper magic good for nothing

but for the good boy soldier
the best was a tattoo
in an ink mixed of human bile
and the peeled skin of a monk,
or better still
a desiccated human foetus
cut from the uterus of a woman
pregnant three months;

the protector on a string
who would always whisper
advice and encouragement
through the din
of dangerous times;

a tiny, shrivelled thing
cleaving close to his heart, or held
between his teeth, as
the enemy charged in.

Aubade 6

I wake you up
just to know
you dream

of that other man
you meet in them

in the dark, in that still
dawn cool.

I wake you up
to show you this
when the lights come up.

And you'll say
'Of course darling, it was you.'

If I met him there
what would I do

when it's still too dark
to know.

'Tell me about him,' I'd ask,
'what he's got
that I haven't

and if it's really me
and if the scenery's
still that good
at the moment of waking.'

Pol Pot in Paris

Oh happy child, kindly teacher – were you a fake?
Like you I'm taciturn
but when I give an order who's to hear?
Paris, I found it cold but didn't read very much.
No-one knows what you thought of its weather,
the river, the churches or the metro.
You preferred a book on the Soviets to girls
    in Montmartre.
I too would rather recite Verlaine
than take notes on electronics.
If I had a history and traditions, I don't remember.
Would you understand me?
I too lived on an allowance
of uncomfortable epithets
cobbled from Buddha and Marx:
'Physical beauty is an obstacle to the will to struggle.'

Late nights drinking weren't your thing.
Sweet words of girls 'mask evil hearts'.
A fun holiday on a tractor in Belgrade.
'The wheels of revolution never stop, roll on
to crush all who dare to walk in its path.'
We could have been lifetime friends, together
rooting out evil, picking mushrooms,
sipping coffee in the Latin Quarter,

mediocre, polite, soft spoken
migrants meandering in overcoats.

The others marry French girls, you join a work brigade
digging ditches in Zagreb.
In the 15th arrondissement, Rue Latellier
mid-winter, dog shit everywhere.
On the river it's 20 francs
for *La Grande Revolution Française*.
We could've talked, taken notes for a memoir:
did you join the party before or after the festival
in East Berlin? Did you buy that shirt
before or after the coup d'état?

In Marseille you boarded the *Jamaique*.
Your tiny shadow cast a conspiracy
of epic dimensions, and there, in the oily backwash
and the silver wake, a complete solution.
I too went home, dreaming of a family
I would never have, and the one I would.

Letter to Marguerite Duras

The white trash girl in the second hand Fedora,
hardly fifteen, waits at the convent school gate.
(Once I taught a girl like you, from Hanoi, and rich.)
A *Morris Léon Bollée*, black, appears;
at the wheel a white liveried driver.
On the concession it's flat, sad, futureless.
A view of the mountains of Siam,
an oppressive heat of course.
Just like here, where I am writing this
sending your book back to you
across a sluggish canal of memory, writing to you.
White trash on a concession
and two brothers drunk on Cognac and Pastis,
one a killer, the other mostly mute.
A mother who's lost her husband
in a way that's not explained.

What else can I say, I love the way
the Chinese lover could never have you
and how he made love with a kind of grace
you'd call French if you believed it were true.
And there was Hélène Lagonelle
with her arms thrown up in surrender
sleeping with her legs apart
under the dormitory fan, just turning over, lazily.
I love the inversion, you were poor

and he was rich, his fate determined, an Oriental.
The way he sat there, head averted from humility,
in the back seat of the car.

I am him, I am you, and everyone's talking about it.
No, there's no point standing on the steamer's deck
looking back down the river
to Saigon, slowly disappearing under the horizon.
Nothing's explained, which is why
we're slumped in the deckchairs, always reading.
Moral decay, a quagmire
leading to persistent drinking.
The weather's vengeful collaboration.
History ends but love is endless,
dying but undying, always damp
and always just beginning.

Lines from The Lover

It was never a question of beauty but something else. Mind for example. For a long time you had no dress of your own, except those your mother had her servant make. Dô could sew with hair-fine needles, pleats and Peter Pan collars. She could make anything look timeless. Writing was sewing. Writing was taking an image – a ferry crossing the Mekong say, and empty it of all significance until it became idea, an image caught between memory and forgetting. We looked about for that place-marker for the time that never existed. *The Mekong – that blood in the body, that slow flow between banks that had faded away. The river carries everything along, straw huts, forests, burnt-out fires, dead birds, dead dogs, drowned tigers and buffaloes, drowned men, bait, islands of water hyacinths all stuck together. Everything flows towards the Pacific, no time for anything to sink, all is swept along by the deep and headlong storm of the inner current, suspended on the surface of the river's strength.* And like a newborn child, it was blind, or so it seemed to the ungainly, the women from elsewhere, the mothers and the sons, *mute and cowed in the presence of the father*. And it was blind.

The Photo

for Pring Noeuan

And we left
with your final testimony
in our ears.

The way I held my breath to find
knee-deep below us with the sun going down
a moat the colour of old iron

the armless statue of a meditating man
and the living beggar's
arm held out to us.

The war hanging there
quietly blazing – like an argument
waiting for an excuse
to begin again.

Not that you
or anyone that day
had that kind of energy.

Whoever you were
that day at the river
they were now your children, the beauteous students
bathing and pushing, one

on another, mistresses
of the clean body and
the well formed alphabets.

A boat propelled by
ghost and metaphor
rowed past
and then another,
practising pursuit.

Perhaps an evening storm
blew them this way, and
they remain as hauntings,
an imprint
of hands, or maybe oars
however framed
held together
by laughter, tradition
breath or gaze.

So we left the gold leaf there
at Angkor
at the people's inscription

and you recalled a bad year
quietly smouldering.
A beggar held out a cup
and a couple (you and him
engaged in '75)
retraced their steps
in sand.

You, the defenceless writer
engaged (let's say at gunpoint)
to an armed illiterate
standing for the wedding shots
among the stony
monumental litter, posing
for a photo with the headless monsters.

To forget or not to,
to write or not to – therefore *live* –
to *forgive* the monster
is this impossible question.

Those who do not read
are still with us
and so few of you who write
with any skill or beauty.

We move forward, all the same, dear friend
back and forward
across the moat
one more time.

Notes

Nyepi describes a Balinese purification ceremony. At a certain lunar time Bali shuts down for 24 hours in order to fool evil spirits into thinking the island has been abandoned.

The Fire Watchers: A Memoir (in the Sydney Style) echoes Robert Adamson's poem 'My house' in *Where I Come From* (1979): *why did my mother / never sew the hems of my jeans, even if Death on the TV / reminded her of her children?*

Translations From the Malay is a riff on English phrases accompanied by Malay equivalents adapted from a 1930s phrasebook for British colonial administrators serving in Malaya in the 1930s.

A Map of Cambodia: *Where the sugar palms are / you'll find a Cambodian.* The Khmer Rouge believed that the presence of a sugar palm defined the territory of Cambodia.

Siem Reap Dawn, **Forest Wat**, **The War Never Ends**, **Dukkha (Craving)**, and **Songkhran** are responses or 're-writes' of Michelle Cahill's excellent poems in her book, *Accidental Cage* (2007). *Dukkha*: a Buddhist term for suffering or dissatisfaction arising from false consciousness, ignorance, and desire for illusory things.

Silk: A Wearer's Guide: technical aspects of silk making are from Gillian Green, *Traditional Textiles of Cambodia: Cultural Threads and Material Heritage*, River Books, 2003.

Aubade 2: *I wake in old 'Funan' / It was clear to Zhou Da Guan (1296) why /the Khmers never travel at night.* The Chinese name for the Khmer empire was Funan. An emissary from China, Zhou Da Guan left an invaluable, if unreliable, ethnography of late 13th century Khmer culture. His report, *Memoirs on the Customs of Cambodia* has been widely consulted by Cambodia scholars ever since; and *the breaking of the insteps / of wellborn Chinese girls*, is a quote fromTomaž Šalamun's 'Words' in *Feast: Poems*, edited by Charles Simic, Harcourt Inc, 2000.

S21 describes Tuol Sleng prison, in Phnom Penh, now a 'genocide museum'. Between 1975 and 1978 the Khmer Rouge executed about 20 000 of their own cadres in an effort to purge the party of 'enemies from within'. The victims were tortured into signing 'confessions' that would implicate other possible enemies, including their relatives. Of the total number of prisoners, perhaps six survived. The head of the prison was Comrade Duch, a maths teacher, now on trial for genocide.

The 32 Hells describes a bas-relief in Angkor Wat, depicting thirty-two kinds of torture. For an in-depth study, see *Khmer Mythology: Secrets of Angkor*, Vittorio Roveda, River Books, Bangkok, 1997, pp. 106–8.

The Triumph of Sangrama Over the Traitor Kamvau. Sangrama was the leading general under the 11th century Khmer king Udayadityavarman II. The battle between the Sangrama and Kamvau is described on a stele at Preah Ngok. My source is an English translation by Claude Jacques of a French translation by Auguste Barth, in Claude Jacques, *Angkor: Cities and Temples*, River Books, Bangkok, 1997, pp. 136–8.

Dear Henri: Henri Mouhot (1826–1861) was an Anglo-French explorer and naturalist who has been accredited with the European 'discovery' of Angkor Wat. He died of jungle fever trying to reach Luang Prabang, Laos. His journal *Travels in Siam, Cambodia, Laos, and Annam* is published by White Lotus Press, Bangkok, 2000.

Louis De Carné's Diary, subtitled *Travels in Indo-China and the Chinese Empire* describes the work of the Colonial French Mekong Exploration Commission (1886–1888). It is a mix of travel diary and trade report, and a guide to French colonial policy in Indochina. De Carné predicted that India would fall into the hands of the Australians. He considered Indochina's climate too enervating for whites, and described

Annam (Vietnam) as a 'counting house'. In his introduction, De Carné wrote: 'by a kind of natural law, which one can hardly admit without sadness, there is scarcely an alternative, for races outside European civilisation, between a melancholy transformation, or a remorseless extinction.' For the English translation, see *Travels on the Mekong, Cambodia, Laos and Yunnan*, White Lotus, Bangkok, 2000.

For the River and the Spring Again is partly a response to 'Bird in an Empty City', by Meng Jiao (751–814), in *Meng Jiao, Classical and Contemporary Poets in Parallel*, translated by Kit Kelen, Hilda Tam, and Amy Wong, ASM Poetry, Macao 2007.

Poem consists of Khmer proverbs. *Revolutionaries must be pulled from the earth like diamonds* was a favourite slogan of the Khmer Rouge.

Aubade 5 (Bishma on a bed of arrows): Bishma is a warrior-king from the Kauravas (sons of Darkness), who were enemies of the Pandavas (sons of Light) in the Mahabharata. Mortally wounded, but of semi-divine origin, he could choose the time of his own death.

Letter to Marguerite Duras, and **Lines from The Lover** scramble quotations from Duras' autobiographical novella *L'Amant*, translated by Barbara Bray, Random House 1985.